MICHELLE CABLING & GNOEY PEAT

Crash Landing On You Book

A Review Of Korean TV Drama Masterpiece

This book was professionally typeset on Reedsy.
Find out more at reedsy.com

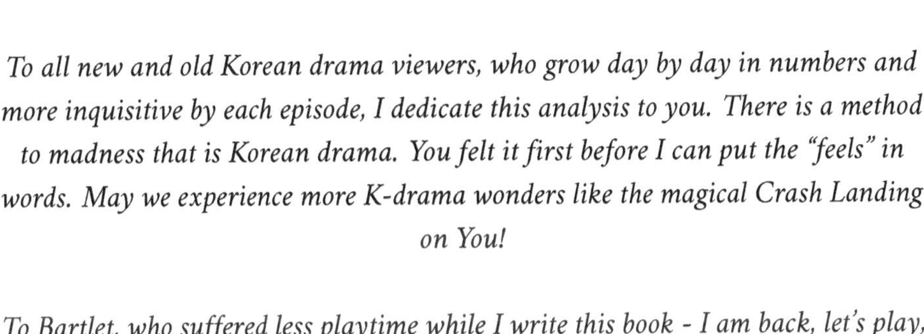

To all new and old Korean drama viewers, who grow day by day in numbers and more inquisitive by each episode, I dedicate this analysis to you. There is a method to madness that is Korean drama. You felt it first before I can put the "feels" in words. May we experience more K-drama wonders like the magical Crash Landing on You!

To Bartlet, who suffered less playtime while I write this book - I am back, let's play, play.

"The best and most beautiful things in the world cannot be seen or even touched - they must be felt with the heart."

- HELEN KELLER

Contents

Preface

Critics tend to look down on TV drama as sub-par to films. Asian drama was perceived to be soapy, with a predictable script, low-grade production value and lame acting. Nevertheless, no one can deny that the world has changed. As a category, TV drama series has improved in many ways, alongside the public's increasing taste for compelling, fresh storytelling. Many are getting tired of the usual sex and violence. Compared to film, a TV series demands more time-investment from its audience than a regular two-hour film. The bigger-the-louder-the-better formula now seems too old and cliché as viewers have grown wise.

Korean drama, for one, offers a clean alternative to the mainstream fuel. It contains beautiful stories usually weaving in drama, action, comedy, fantasy, suspense, and comedy in one TV series. More Korean drama are now of high production value even with weekly broadcast (which translates to tight deadline). New avenues of distribution like Netflix, Rakuten, and Viu (and other free sites) led to global reach for K-dramas. During Covid-19 pandemic period, K-drama reaped new patrons as many people discovered it while mainly staying at home during lockdowns.

It warrants more public discourse as to its influence on mainstream cultures especially outside South Korea. It deserves more serious discussion and examination of its overall impact on relevant conversations of our time. This way, it will continue to improve and elevate its standard and produce higher quality series. May this book inspires every K-drama viewer, not just to feel, but to think of what is good in every series they watch and voice out what they think can be improved further. It is the only way for these beloved K-dramas, not only to survive, but to thrive and stay for long. - Michelle Cabling, Author

Acknowledgement

Sending a heartfelt gratitude to the cast and crew, producer, writer, director and everyone who were involved and worked on Crash Landing On You. If ever this humble book reaches you, please write your name on the blank below.

Thank you very much,

————————————————————

for being part of the masterpiece series -

"Crash Landing On You"

One

Magnum Opus Scriptor

❧

SCRIPT WRITTEN BY PARK JI-EUN

The Story and its First Hook

A chaebol[1] heiress, Yoon Se-ri, crash-landed in a North Korean village due to a paragliding mishap. "Crash Landing On You" tells the story of her quest to return home. She literally (and figuratively) falls into the arms of a North Korean military captain, the reticent Ri Jeong Hyeok. Also known as Captain Ri (Lee), he wills to do everything to protect her and keep her safe from danger. A love story doomed from the outset because of the protracted war between countries; hence, the improbable happy-ever-after conclusion made it more exciting to pursue the series.

Park Ji-Eun treated viewers to a double storyline in this 16-episode series that carefully intertwined and cohesively stitched as one solid story. The first half (1-9 episodes) narrates how Yoon Se-ri tried to go back to South Korea while the remaining half focuses on Captain Ri (Lee) protecting Yoon Se-ri. It is a familiar plot, and some may say pedestrian, as a romantic story

---

[1] a family-controlled industrial conglomerate in South Korea: *Source: Merriam Webster Dictionary*

of ill-starred lovers fighting against all odds. The female lead character's main desire was to go back to South Korea. The narrative revolved around the countless barriers leading to many failed attempts of returning to Seoul. The simplicity of protagonists' goal laced with tricky obstacles in between makes it a riveting story to pursue. A North Korean man and South Korean woman ordained to cross path for destiny to unfold and the notorious Mr Fate descending to their lives is an intriguing hook.

Image source credit: Netflix – Yoon Se-ri fell from the tree to Captain Lee/Ri's arms after she crash-landed in North Korea. A North & South Korean encounter is the first major hook of "Crash Landing On You.

Caught up in North Korea, the protagonist's high stake plight drew the crowd to this series. A valid predicament that viewers can relate to easily. Many of us have little recognisance of life in North Korea, let alone the doom of anyone trapped inside its territory. What will you do if you went missing and found yourself in North Korean soil? The audience couldn't help but rally for Yoon Se-ri to make it back in one piece in Seoul. A matter of life and death situation absolutely thrilled the audience. Coupled with the prospect of a promising romance along the road, viewers attention were soaked right from the very start.

Masterfully Curated Scenes

The whole script is no doubt, an intelligently well-written masterpiece. It was neither lazily and hastily written, nor did it take the easy way out of any scenarios. It resulted in lots of one-of-a-kind scenes. With every part adequately thought-of, hardly any scene is expendable. Scenes flew from one to the next with a clever tie-up to a keyword or visual. These smart references show meaningful connection among scenes. It is like being served a chef-d'œuvre[2] where one cannot help but feel respected and dignified. An example of suchsmart linking was when Yoon Se-ri encountered the tornado and went missing. Her office manager Hong Chang-Sik desperately looked out for her. He exclaimed with tears, "How high have you gone up, boss?" The next scene was Yoon Se-ri caught up hanging just on a forest tree - not that high as Hong Chang-Sik words foreshadowed.

Every scenario has a clear purpose of evoking specific emotion from the audience. Every scene is never too long to be tiresome or too short to be futile. It was full of entertainment value but not using usual formula. Viewers are hard-pressed to name the most favourite scene out of the wealth of fresh and memorable scenes..

Unpredictable Twists and Turns Aplenty

"Crash Landing On You" is full of unexpected paths. No one could ever guess how Yoon Se-ri will eventually get out of North Korea, even after many failed attempts. The ending scene of episode 9, for example, finally brought Yoon Se-ri back to South Korea. Still, the kissing scene at the end made the audience think Captain Ri (Lee) was defecting as he crossed the border during the kiss. The next scene shows that Captain Ri (Lee) discovered the hidden

---

[2]   a masterpiece especially in art or literature. *Source: Merriam Webster Dictionary*

message that Yoon Se-ri left in his bookshelves. A proof that he did not defect. The audience eagerly anticipated how the couple would meet again.

Moreover, the more significant questions were how will they even end up together and if they are even to end up together given the insurmountable barrier. The last episode had the most unpredictable point of the series. While both protagonists achieved their goals, it still left the audience rooting for them to be happily living together. Such cornucopia of unanticipated events glued the audience to their sofa week after week. While Korean dramas are known to have such unpredictability, *"Crash Landing On You"* writer Park took it to the highest level, much to the audience's delight.

Sui Generis Scenes

If you have watched many rom-coms, it becomes easy to detect another similar scene is coming. *"Crash Landing On You"* is immensely different from that as it adopted fresh dialogues and never-before-seen conversations aplenty. Furthermore, it did not need any sexual overtones to engage the audience in its story.

All the pouty scenes of Ri Jeong Hyeok classified as sui generis[3]. He did so few times in the series, yet it was not tiresome at all. Like when Ri Jeong Hyeok realised her capitalist nature of Yoon Se-ri's heart. Or when he was pouting after hearing an earful from her regarding his excessive playing of a computer game. Even the couple ring scene, which every other Korean drama would contain, was still written with such spirit of newness. *"Crash Landing On You"* contained a voluminous collection of original scenes that watching it is such a treat.

---

[3]   constituting a class alone : unique, peculiar. *Source: Merriam Webster Dictionary*

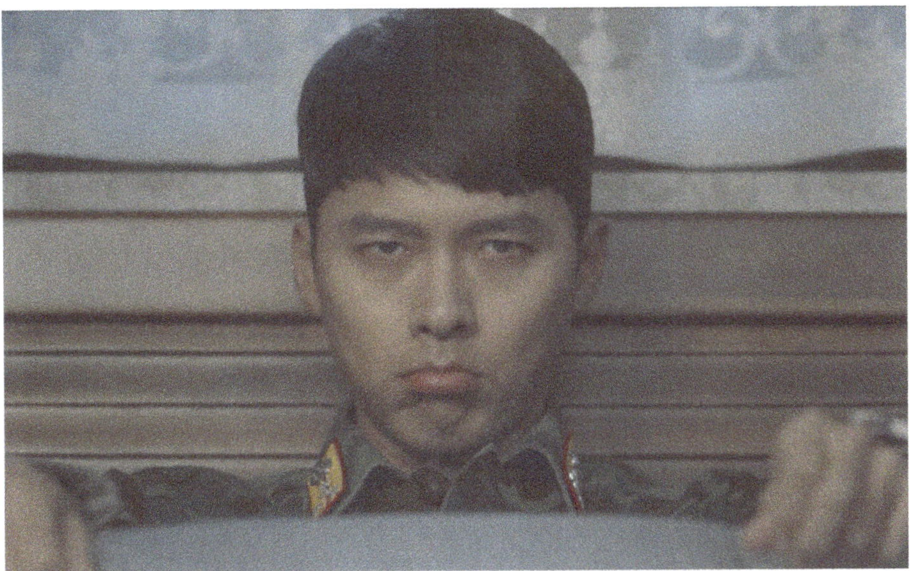

Image source credit to Netflix – Considered sue generis, this is one of the pouting scenes popularised in the hit series

Some of these incredible scenes of its own class are:

Seri's Awarding Ceremony, ep 1

Yoon Seri giving out awards and prizes to the troops was such a sweet and thoughtful gesture on her part. Every soldier's response to the award, and each one's chosen reward, delivered moments of innocence and pure fun. Captain Ri (Lee)'s priceless reaction for not getting an award was very charming. Receiving a special gift from Yoon Se-ri, a tomato plant, he had to nurture by reciting ten nice words every day. It was a beautiful twist he never wanted, nonetheless thoroughly cherished.

Falling into Captains Ri's Arms, ep 1

Yoon Seri's waving both her hands and feet was one original rendition of someone seeking attention from hanging on top of a tree. This particular scene also balanced the tone of the story from a dangerous to a light-hearted one. Son Ye Jin's perfect portrayal of falling off from the tree to the arms of Captain Ri (Lee) was as great as this series gets.

'Unboxing' scene, ep 2

Yoon Se-ri's 'unboxing' a bag full of essential stuff from Captain Ri (Lee) and how he acquired these contrabands from the market was another exciting sequence. Though rarely seen in a comedy project, Son Ye Jin's outstanding comical acting is splendid. Similarly, Captain Ri (Lee)'s awkward and upright character in procuring contrabands was a sure delight.

Fake Your Affection Or Else, ep 2

Yoon Se-ri always pursues what she wants while she remains a lovable character. The situation she created was so trivial—threatening to stay in the village if Captain Ri (Lee) does not fake warm affection in front of the neighbours. Captain Ri (Lee) was so at his element of being stoic in response to petty demands of Yoon Se-ri, which turned him into a more endearing character.

Succinctly-Written Story Arcs

Story arcs represent the *scene flow* from the beginning, rising action, climax, falling action, and ending. In episodic series, each episode tends to follow a story arc or the rise and fall of tension as the story flow. In *"Crash Landing On You,"* each episode ends in a cliffhanger. Zeigarnik effect[4] kicks in and viewers wait earnestly for the continuation. The mind will not forget the unresolved task or story, making final endings with open interpretation for the audience is never a great idea in delighting the viewing public.

---

[4]   the psychological tendency to remember an uncompleted task rather than a completed one.
Source - Merriam Webster Dictionary for Medicine

Cliffhanger Endings

Will she be punished?
Yoon Se-ri crash-landed in North Korea territory. As she tried to return back to South Korea, she failed miserably

1

Yoon Se-ri ended up being discovered by the merciless officer
Will she be punished?

2

3
Yoon Se-ri forged a plan with the North Koreans, but failed and instead, got caught
Will she be punished?

4 Yoon- Se-ri was lost in the market
Will she be mentally strong to escape back to Seoul?

Captain Ri was shot
Will he die? **6**

Captain Ri caught a man holding Yoon Se-ri in the elevator **5**
Is she in danger?

Yoon Se-ri's secret was revealed to Seo Dan, the captain's fiancée
7 Will Yoon Se-ri be revealed and punished now?

8 Yoon Se-ri was taken away
Will she die?

Yoon Se-ri finally went back to Seoul
Will they ever meet again? **9**

Ri Jeong Hyeok sneaked in South Korea **10**
Will he be caught?

11 The villain was after Yoon Se-ri
Will Yoon Se-ri be in serious danger?

12 Yoon Se-ri was letting Ri Jeong Hyeok go
Will she be fine?

Yoon Se-ri got shot
Will she die? **13**

Captain Ri found the villain but South Korea authorities also caught them
Will he get punished? **14**

Yoon Se-ri's health turned for the worse
15 Will she die?

Yoon Se-ri and Jeong Hyeok saw each other again in Switzerland after three years
Will it be a happy ever after? **16**

Each story arc in "*Crash Landing On You*" is so well-paced. The situation development in every episode is significant enough to avoid humdrum, which leads to viewer disinterest usually caused by the slow pace. The writers never took any episode for granted and ensured that the high writing quality was consistent throughout. Every episode's high positive reception is not just a stroke of luck in a few scenes that worked out. Excellence in writing at every turn leads the audience along the path where they have no choice but to follow along where the writer takes them joyfully.

Perfect Pacing

Viewers are masters when it comes to detecting slow pacing of story. They will sense it quickly, and that is the critical point that they will disengage from inhabiting the world she/he is watching. With a long 16-episode of 70-minute each length series (except for the 16th episode with 120 minutes), the pacing is critical. The audience will lose excitement or worse, leave the series if it is too slow or gets confused when it is too fast. "*Crash Landing On You*" is nothing short of a well-fine-tuned balance.

Each episode is sure to provide progress of the character's goal and resolves one, giving rise to another tension toward the end, while setting up the first scene for the succeeding episode. It has never been slow or fast in its story development, even with many other characters telling its own story. The finale episode runs much longer, about 120 minutes, and is comparable to an average film. Nevertheless, there was no sense that it was an extended episode as the tying up of each character's arc flew naturally.

Witty Dialogues

The ultimate measure of excellent dialogues is when viewers vividly recall these scenes and in some cases, can recite the actual lines. The dilemma in preparing conversations is between the proper use of relatable but not alien-sounding lines while not employing predictable, snooze-inducing exchanges. It has to be probable, yet unexpected; possible yet unforeseeable. In short, it has to be written impeccably for a discerning audience. Each line in *"Crash Landing On You"* was written with an explicit purpose and in most instances, connected to another scene in the previous or future episode. Writer Park is just so prolific in linking dialogues into cohesive, tight storytelling.

It is also challenging to be effective in many genres within just one series. The more focus on one genre a script is, theoretically, the better. *"Crash Landing On You"* delivers excellent writing that flawlessly conveyed heart-pumping chase and action, comedic relief, romantic moments, and drama that fills up buckets of tears. Viewers' hearts raced with intense action scenes, laughed a lot at the comedy, ecstatic for the loving couple, and cried their hearts out for every painful scene. Only a handful of Korean series delivered this much, this great.

Here are some of the dialogues that elicited spontaneous emotions from the audience.

Priceless Comedy

In episode 2, Yoon Se-ri is cleverly forcing Capt Ri to fake his affection toward her in front of the neighbours. She mischievously threatens him of not leaving North Korea and just getting married to him since he is her ultimate type. Not only because Capt Ri is doing it while in full display of shame, but also on the unutterable reaction of people who are seeing a taboo made it so hilarious. Yoon Se-ri is not affected by their response and joyfully hops back to the house with a great sense of achievement.

Image source credit to Netflix | The scene where Yoon Se-ri is threatening Captain Ri (Lee) to fake a warm affection toward her is one of the funniest scenes in "Crash Landing On You"

Yoon Se-ri: "We're engaged anyway, so we might as well just get married. I told you, your face is totally my type."

Capt Ri dreadfully touches her hair.

Yoon Se-ri: "Olaa (gosh, Honey!)" And gives out a very naughty smile.

Captain Ri (Lee): "I'm leaving."

In episode 4, Capt Ri had to confide with the two soldiers, Pyo Chi Su and Kim Ju-Myeok, after receiving a hand heart from Yoon Se-ri. Probing about what the gesture meant, he was consequently horrified to know the symbol's real meaning. Pyo Chi Su assured him not to worry because "it is not like he is married or engaged." Captain Ri (Lee)'s face could not deny the fact that he is engaged to be married. The soldiers exclaimed in unison, *You do?"*

Seo Dan's mother and uncle were an awesome comedic team-up in episode 5. Captain Ri (Lee) ended up driving Seo Dan back to Pyongyang and forced to have dinner with Seo Dan's family.

Capt Ri: "It's been a while. I'm sorry for coming this late."

Dan's mother: "Don't say that. It's not late at all.

What's late is your marriage."

At the dinner table:

Dan's mother: "All the matchmakers somehow figured out that Dan came back from Russia and begged me that they would like to see her just once. I told them she's already engaged, but they were so persistent."

Uncle: "Persistent? Who is? I mean, I just have never heard about this."

Captain Ri (Lee)'s father also displayed some potent comical bombs in episode 9. Even though his character was a serious, military man, his conversation with Yoon Se-ri was fun filled.

Father: "So tell me, what is your purpose in approaching Ri Jeong Hyeok and staying with him?"

Yoon Se-ri: "Purpose? That's absolutely unfair."

"Sir, please think about it. I'm running a company in South Korea...this might sound like bragging, but we have 14 stores overseas. Why would I go here to put myself in trouble? I am just an innocent citizen of Seoul who has been worrying about what I should do with all that money, and if I will ever get to use all the money before I die."

Spectacular Epilogues

"Crash Landing On You" writer also crafted powerful epilogues. These added extra scenes made the story juicier and more intriguing. It is a brilliant move to show another angle from a previously shown scene or a relevant flashback. It whets viewers' appetite for more episodes.

Episode 1 – This epilogue is very special as it confirms that Yoon Se-ri made Ri Jeong Hyeok's heart flutter. He allowed himself to let out a smile even before meeting her. At that time, Ri Jeong Hyeok has lived his life devoid of potential happiness due to his brother's untimely death.

Episode 2 – Yoon Se-ri and Ri Jeong Hyeok were in the same place in Switzerland precisely at the same time around seven years ago. Both were standing side by side, watching the paragliders in an exhibition. To which they both exclaimed "whoa" in awe. It was a revelation to the audience that they encountered each other in the past in another country.

Episode 3 – Ri Jeong Hyeok was reciting ten nice words to care for the tomato plant. Nostalgia enveloped Ri Jeong Hyeok as he says the word "piano." It was simple yet brilliant acting of Hyun Bin to recite positive words, yet imbibed sadness, hope, and longing all at the same time.

Image source credit to Netflix | The epilogue where Captain Ri (Lee) reciting ten words to the tomato tree

"*Sea.*

   Sunlight.

Azalea.
Dewdrop.
Fleecy Cloud.
Calico Cat.
Rose.
Breeze.
First Snow.
Piano."

Epilogue 4 – Yoon Se-ri and Ri Jeong Hyeok finally met face to face on a Switzerland bridge. It was the exact spot where Se-ri was planning to jump off the bridge. At which point, Ri Jeong Hyeok asked her to take pictures of him and Seo Dan, thereby stopping her from jumping off the bridge.

Epilogue 7 – Ri Jeong Hyeok played the piano at the port near lake Iseltwald, Switzerland. He played the song that he wrote for his brother for the first time. Yoon Se-ri heard the song when she was contemplating about her life, which the song served as a solace to her when she decided to continue living.

Epilogue 9 – Ri Jeong Hyeok found a heart-warming message on his books on the shelves that Yoon Se-ri re-arranged to read "I Love You, Ri Jeong Hyeok." It also signalled that he did not defect to South Korea.

Epilogue 12 – Ri Jeong Hyeok heard the recording of Yoon Se-ri and remembered the moment in Switzerland. He realised then that fate indeed brought them together.

Epilogue 14 – Ri Jeong Hyeok recorded the song "Song for my Brother" as he played it in piano. He asked her to play the recorder whenever she could not sleep instead of taking sleeping pills. He also stocked up her pantry of healthy ingredients, telling her that they should live like they will see each other again the next day. It is a foreshadowing of the inevitable – that he will eventually leave South Korea.

Epilogue 15 – The couple enjoyed a walk in the park under the rain in Seoul. A scene where they enjoyed each other's company and as a sweet couple spending time together.

Beautiful Ending

Great endings are never about a happy or sad fate of the characters. That is a given and expected based on the values reflected in the story (justice for good, punishment for the bad). What is important is how one arrives at the ending that is satisfying to the viewing public. Getting the ending right is a massive challenge in Korean dramas. Many started great but fell flat in giving a satisfying, well-deserved closure. With the audience investing 16-30 hours to watch one whole series, it raises a very high expectation to deliver a fulfilling ending. Nowadays, viewers leave comments on what they think and feel about the series in real-time online. Such feedbacks affect the overall reception and performance of the series.

It is a delicate balance of bringing an ending that is acceptable and satisfying but not in any way predictable. *"Crash Landing On You"* provided a stunning and unanticipated conclusion. The main couple was shown in breathtaking visuals in the ending scene using Switzerland's alps and greeneries as a gorgeous backdrop. Viewers remember *Crash Landing On You's* ending as a stunning, exquisite scene of the lead couple finally living happily ever after.

Crash Landing On You's conclusion threads on the delicate line between a great and an awful ending. It pivoted the conversation on a second season look-out. No one wanted this series to end. It creatively resolved that the couple finally got together. However, at the same time, it did not settle it traditionally through cliche endings of a wedding or having children narrative. It left viewers room to interpret the last few scenes. If viewers saw a marriage or children cues at the ending, they will be pleased, but will quickly forget about the series as the brain thinks it resolved the tension. However, the brain cannot forget something unresolved (remember Zeigarnik effect) such as – do the couple only meet then for two weeks in a year?

Image source credit: Netflix | The ending of Crash Landing On You full of exquisite visuals

A lot has been said and written about what exactly the ending implied. However, the key was in the visual design of the last three minutes of the final episode. Before the last scene, the couple held hands discreetly while watching a concert in Switzerland, where they meet two weeks every year. The 16th epilogue rolled as Se-ri gathering picnic items around the house. This house showcased many picture frames of the couple, seemingly one for the past two years they have been meeting for the two-week annual holiday. The villa seemed a permanently inhabited place; else, picture frames will not be a fixture. She went up to the hill to join Ri Jeong Hyeok, who was walking there with a stem of white flowers in his hand. She added this to her vase of pink flowers, and he hugged her close to him. Unlike the discrete holding of hands in the previous scene, this last scene showed they are out in the open, having a picnic. Finally, there were signs of freedom to be together, and they are not afraid to be seen together anymore. The end was a final sweet kiss as they watched the sunset together. A careful look at the visuals tells the story as it is – a happy ever after.

"Crash Landing On You" also wrapped up other characters' story in socially accepted themes. Such as good deeds take on a prize, bad gets punished in

the end, and most of all, justice and love always prevail.

While the audience can separate truth from fiction, the permeability of Korean dramas in the mainstream has the power to affect society's capacity to normalise behaviours or ideas. For this alone, *"Crash Landing On You"* deserves high praise on how it propelled good over destructive behaviours. Moreover, it proved to be successful without resorting to mature interests like sex or violence. Instead, it gives a fresh take on familiar themes like integrity, friendship, respect for others, and community engagement.

* * *

Two

Beloved People, Not Just Characters

riter Park Ji-Eun's brilliance created "endearing people" in *"Crash Landing On You"* and not mere characters. Aside from the wise and fresh dialogues, characters' buildout in the series is another golden feather that turns the series into a masterpiece. The writing thoroughly focused on the main characters, Yoon Se-ri and Ri Jeong Hyeok. The series' concentration on their main story is integral to the series' overall allure. Its singularity of focus sustained audience pursuit as story with too many subplots tend to not go deep.

Furthermore, the writer also capably launched another second couple to cheer for. It also served lovesome and winning characters with exciting stories of their own. These secondary characters are vital in endearing the series to the viewers. It would not be a captivating series without heralding their values and struggles. Beyond character creation, writer Pak Ji-Eun cleverly balanced the demands of romance, action, comedy, suspense, and drama in a Korean drama series. The *dramatis personnae* made *"Crash Landing On You"* a timeless, beautiful story of people from "near yet far" corners of the world.

Yoon Se-ri

Yoon Se-ri is a South Korean chaebol heiress, who paraglided to test her parachutes line, but accidentally crash-landed in North Korea after encountering a tornado. She is wealthy in her way, a successful mogul who started and achieved success in her business. She is known to be a demanding boss who can be stubborn and arrogant at times. Her family relationship is troubled, given the pressures of the family business' succession battle against her brothers. She grew up with a father and a complicated relationship with her stepmother. With a life devoid of any other close and meaningful relationship, she battled depression, anxiety, and suicidal tendencies.

She is not a damsel in distress. Granted that she landed in a place far from her familiar environment, Yoon Se-ri is not one who needed a man to be successful. As a conglomerate family daughter, she proved herself to be successful in her own right by starting a business and expanding it into a large company. This impressive feat convinced her father to name her the next leader of the conglomerate, much to his brothers' chagrin.

Image source credit to Netflix | Yoon Se-ri is a power woman character. This scene shows her reaction when her father declared her as the next CEO of the family conglomerate.

Se-ri shattered the highest glass ceiling from an upheld family tradition in South Korea - that the first son gets to inherit and lead the family business. She might have been born with a silver spoon. However, she also has real-life issues. She developed mental anguish, anxiety, and depression, which led her to seek refuge in Switzerland to undergo euthanasia. She is like an average person with many life's challenges and, at one point, ready to give up her meaningless life. She managed to turn around her perspective and resolved to do something better than ending her life – launching her own business with great success. She just wanted to grow and do better on what she chose to do in life – the most recent, a chance to lead her family's conglomerate and make her father proud.

Even when she ended up in a North Korean village, she used her capability and wit to find ways to return to South Korea unscathed. On her first encounter with Captain Ri (Lee), she was able to run fast, albeit in the wrong direction, to save herself from the chase. As soon as it dawned on her that money and influence cannot help her escape, she quickly adapted to her environment. She learned to cooperate with the soldiers to earn favour from them. She forced Captain Ri (Lee) and his comrades to help her escape back to South Korea. She even turned around the ajummas on her side, despite her image as a 'national treasure' stealer.

She endeared herself to the four soldiers of Captain Ri (Lee), who later risked their lives to save her. She even managed herself well in front of Seo Dan's, the captain's fiancée, during confrontations. She forced Captain Ri (Lee) to publicly show off his affection for her while threatening him with indefinite stay unless he does what she asks – in a humorous way. Yoon Se-ri remained clear and steadfast about her main goal of returning to South Korea when she would face Captain Ri (Lee)'s father.

Once back in her country, she was able to stop her relatives from taking over her business and rewarded those who were loyal to her (i.e., the insurance agent). She saved Captain Ri (Lee) twice from Cho Cheol Gang – in the parking lot chase, and when he was about to be reshot, she used her car as a shield to protect him, consequently getting shot instead. Even at the demarcation line, she thought not to let go of Ri Jeong Hyeok for fear that terrible things might happen to him, all because of her. Yoon Se-ri is not a damsel in distress – far from it. She represented a modern, thinking, and powerful woman who stood for her values and fought for her loved ones. And she does it with her brain and lots of flairs.

She is a woman of continuous refinement. She started as a spoiled, rich lady poised to conquer the business world, but then, she landed in the most vulnerable situation inside North Korea. Like any other person, she cried about the unbelievable fate she encountered, but dusted up and moved on with her goal list. She adapted, utilised what in front of her and worked hard. She had to build rapport with the head of ajummas to get Captain Ri (Lee) a preferential star. She appreciated the things that were quite different from what she'd known like the kimchi cellar or the many uses of bar soap. She expressed her gratitude when she gave out awards to the soldiers and finger hearts when they got physically beaten. Later on, she named her seasonal line of products after the ajummas of the North Korean village whom she came to love and cherish. She is also the first to declare her love for Ri Jeong Hyeok – nothing is braver than expressing love to a North Korean soldier.

Yoon Se-ri's perfect ending. She deserved to be with Captain Ri (Lee). She had to do the gruelling work and waited patiently to meet Ri Jeong Hyeok again. Even in the end, she decided on what she wanted and what she stood for. She spent a wonderful time in a beautiful place with the love of her life – in the end, there is nothing more than Yoon Se-ri deserves than to live happily ever after.

Ri Jeong Hyeok / Captain Ri (Lee)

Ri Jeong Hyeok is a North Korean elite soldier captain assigned to protect the border (DMZ) and lives in a military house in a North Korean village. He is well-respected in the village, even with his reserved personality.

He is from a well-off military family but prefers to keep his lineage private. After his older brother died in a mysterious car accident, he became the only son of the General Police Bureau Director. He used to be a piano student in Switzerland and even spoke multiple languages. He has an opposite temperament than Yoon Se-ri's, which made for a good watch.

Captain Ri (Lee) is the quintessential character that is ultimately THE perfect man. At the outset, he is a character with strong integrity. From the first episode, his honouring of his promise to South Korean soldiers is quite remarkable. He is very considerate and a true gentleman. He did not allow Seo Dan to drive back to Pyongyang on her own because of the dangers involved in driving at night and offered to go with her. He also warned one of the soldiers to deny knowing the accident's details that may endanger the soldier's life. Ri Jeong Hyeok has a strong love for his family and worked hard to obtain justice for his brother's death. He also has a high sense of duty to his country that even when he fell in love with Yoon Se-ri, he never deserted the north.

He was consistently clear on where he stood in many aspects. He was respectful and considerate of his fiancée, Seo Dan, even if he was fully aware that he did not have any romantic feelings for her. Marrying her is only regard for a sense of duty. Once he was sure about his feelings for Yoon Se-ri, he told Seo Dan to halt the wedding. Sadly for Seo Dan, he never misled her for any affection. He did not play mind games. He even told Yoon Se-ri, albeit in the presence of alcohol influence, that he wanted to marry her, stay with her, and have children together. As a result, Yoon Se-ri never doubted his love for her. Their relationship revolved around loving and protecting each other devoid of those self-inflicted and jealousy issues.

Image source credit to Netflix | Ri Jeong Hyeok, a North Korean soldier, became the ultimate protector of the South Korean Yoon Se-ri.

He is THE ultimate protector. It does not hurt that he is an elite soldier, but Captain Ri (Lee) is the best' bodyguard' in town. He could not surrender Yoon Se-ri to the authorities because he did not trust she will get fair treatment. He made up great lies to save her from trouble. For example, he declared

Yoon Se-ri as his fiancée in front of a superior. His thinking was steps ahead of every move like the double-layer of protection when sending her to the airport. He knew too well how to dismantle spy cameras. He was skilful in fighting and even climbed out of a tunnel for many days to reach South Korea to protect Se-ri from Cho Cheol Gang's threat.

Ri Jeong Hyeok, the perfect romantic partner. His love language was sure of service. He looked after Yoon Se-ri's nourishment as he cooks noodles from scratch and grounds granules for his hand-drip coffee to cure her hangover. He prepared a celebration for her birthday and gets a (couple ring) gift. He filled her pantry with essential food and wrote her instructions on how to cook noodles. He recorded himself playing a piano piece so she can sleep well without the aid of sleeping pills. He stayed beside her without eating or sleeping when she was sick. He helped her with small and big things. He sent her timed-messages for a year when he will not be around anymore. He found a way to be with Yoon Se-ri, forever.

Ri Jeong Hyeok sheds the cold and wears the warmth in the end: His character progression was mainly from a withdrawn to a warm personality, from living indifferently to finding purpose in life again. He lost his sweet, friendly demeanour when his brother died and developed a stone cold attitude. Despite this, his goodness and kindness were still within him, and these core values unravelled once he met Yoon Se-ri. After his brother's death, whom he deeply loved, his only way to survive this deep wound was by avoiding any further meaningful relationship.

However, this changed upon meeting Yoon Se-ri. His guards fell, and little by little started to appreciate life again, letting little smiles now and then. He was always conscious of his mistakes and even tried harder to make up for them. He bought Se-ri illegal shampoo and hair conditioner after an afternoon of phone calls insisting on the universal use of soap to no avail. He brewed hand-dripped coffee after a night of drinking to ease her hangover. He even cooked noodles from scratch after chasing her in the forest. After his surgery, he kissed her to make up for shouting at her and misunderstanding her.As Yoon Se-ri also developed feelings for him, both affection grew further alongside Ri Jeong Hyeok's softening outer shell. He allowed his gentle and sweet demeanour that he used to have to resurface. He expressed his deep affection for her in many ways, including the couple's ring birthday gift and the revelation of his true feelings over shots of soju. His actions were well thought-off like when he planned Yoon Se-ri's escape or on how they could meet again in the future. He sent her potted seeds of Edelweiss, which grows commonly in Switzerland, to let her know where they can eventually meet again. In the end, he fulfilled his promise, found Yoon Se-ri after a few years, and spent quality time in a beautiful place with her, ever after.

Seo Dan and Gu Seung Ju/Alberto Gu

Seo Dan is a North Korean heiress and an aspiring cellist engaged to be married to Ri Jeong Hyeok as arranged by their parents. After studying overseas, she returned to North Korea to find her fiancee aiding and falling in love with a South Korean. She contemplated on her upcoming marriage but met Gu Seung Ju, and learned a thing or two about real love.

Gu Seung Ju is a South Korean clever and charming con-man, who came back to South Korea to exact revenge for Se-ri's family. He embezzled money from Se-ri's brother and hid in North Korea, where he met her again. He also met Seo Dan in North Korea - the one he found himself risking his own life to protect.

Seo Dan & Gu Seung Ju –This second couple lead and their character background were also beautifully written. The audience similarly cheered and hoped for their happy ending. Seo Dan is a convincing character, who kept Ri Jeong Hyeok away from Yoon Se-ri (and from the trouble she brings), rightfully so as her fiancée. Her poise and fierceness kept everyone at bay. She is from a wealthy and influential family in North Korea. She is used to getting what she wants, including being betrothed to her first crush, Ri Jeong Hyeok. Seo Dan was troubled by several appearances of Yoon Se-ri with Ri Jeong Hyeok. After insisting on meeting with both their parents, a date was set for their wedding.

Her complete confidence as a woman, who is about to marry the guy she has always loved, was on a high and her fate is back on track. She learned that Ri Jeong Hyeok was in the hospital, and during her visit, he told her that they could not get married anymore as he feels for someone else. Her world crumbled down, but she focused on her goal and insisted that this revelation was not going to break off their wedding. She fully knew that Yoon Se-ri would be leaving soon and hoped that 'feeling' would be gone, too. Seo Dan was every bit the practical and realistic one. When Ri Jeong Hyeok continued to help Yoon Se-ri, Seo Dan chose to reveal this secret to his military father. She decided on this than to phone in a government hotline, which she knew she could not control. However, she broke down after a conversation with Ri Jeong Hyeok inside the prison. He showed her that he was 100% concerned about Se-ri and not a bit about their upcoming wedding.

She met Gu Seung Ju when she was miserable, and he made her realise that Ri Jeong Hyeok never loved her. Though the romance with Gu Seung Ju was short-lived, it was more meaningful than she had ever have gotten from Ri Jeong Hyeok. She eventually realised that she was happy all by herself, chasing her passion in life than chasing someone else who does not have an ounce of love for her. That is how strong a character she was.

On the other hand, Gu Seung Ju had lived a hard life in Britain after Se-ri's father caused his own father's downfall. All he had in his heart was revenge against Yoon Se-ri's family. His plan to take over from the inside of Seri's family by marrying into the family disappeared when Se-ri will not marry him. He resorted to the next best thing and embezzled money from one of her brothers. He succeeded in carrying that out, but as a consequence, he needed to hide where money cannot find him – in North Korea. However, meeting Seo Dan changed everything. He began to see how his life must change and intended to carve out his life anew and be worthy of Seo Dan in the future. However, Gu Seung Ju chose to protect her from the Chinese men chasing him. Sadly, he lost his life in the encounter. Many viewers were affected by his character's death – did he deserve to be killed off after redeeming his flawed character?

Image source credit to TvN | The second lead couple, which is another North-South inter-relations, who both found a common enemy and mutual love in the series.

These two characters certainly gave more depth to the story, and intertwining their lives was a brilliant writing stroke. Kudos to the writer for providing viewers with another couple to love and not waste two enormously charming characters to be just regular villains. Instead, they turned them into endearing anti-heroes, which indeed entered the gates of heaven in the end.

North Korean Soldiers

Pyo Chi-Su – Park Gwang-Beom – Kim Ju-Meok – Geum Eun-Dong

The 'four comrades' is what everyone calls the ultimate squad. Their loyalty to Captain Ri (Lee) and Yoon Se-ri was commendable, risking their lives to help the couple. Each of their characters enriched the team's overall appeal. As a whole, they demonstrated the value of working as a team like overcoming many obstacles to find Captain Ri (Lee) in Seoul and defend Yoon Se-ri from attackers.

Image source credit to Netflix | North Korean comrades risked their lives for Ri Jeong Hyeok and Yoon Se-ri.

Ju Meok's love for Korean drama always came in handy in bridging understanding between two territories. Their dialogues in the series brought light touches and comedic relief like when they bonded with Yoon Se-ri for the first time over soju and clams. Few tears also came out from viewers' eyes when they said goodbye to Yoon Se-ri in Seoul, especially the last one near the DMZ in the finale episode. The writer strengthened the concept of having genuine friends as part of life's support system through them. It also shows that friends can be found everywhere, even in places where supposed enemies thrive. Their loyalty to their country is also laudable. They still decided to come back even with their remarkable experience in Seoul and continued serving their country as soldiers. *"Crash Landing On You"* is not as sweet, enjoyable, and timeless without these four soldiers.

North Korean Ajummas

Ma Yeong-Ae – Na Wol-Sook – Ya OK-Geum – Hyon Myong-Sun

The ajummas painted the daily life in a North Korean village for the viewers, who most likely had insufficient knowledge about this place. They are regular village neighbours, who are the first to gossip and offer help when one of them is in trouble. They are the first to arrive when bad things happen and the first to laugh when good things betide. When the real fiancée of Ri Jeong Hyeok showed up, They were the first to comfort. They brought drinks and much-needed sympathy to help her get through the horror of the recent encounter. These characters are the closest ones Yoon Se-ri ever had as female friends. The irony of finding these gems in the most unexpected place was a lovely touch from the writer. By accepting Yoon Se-ri to be part of their cliche, they provided a much-needed grounding to her as a person. Without them realising it, they made her feel she can rely on them for matters like relationships.

Image source credit: Netflix | The ajummas from the village who were the best girlfriend Se-ri ever had and certainly added richness to Yoon Se-ri's experience in North Korea.

In contrast to her mother and sisters-in-law, who had no meaningful relationship with Yoon Se-ri, she cherished the ajummas for the lovely and exciting times they spent together. It was very heartfelt that she tried to reach out to them by featuring their faces in her beauty products. She called it 'Saudade', which means yearning for happiness that has passed. It was an ingenious way to convey Yoon Se-ri's true feelings for them. She hoped it would reach their village through the ajummas penchant for cosmetic products. Suffice to say the ajummas were mesmerised by Captain Ri (Lee) until the end and disheartened upon learning that their 'national treasure' is about to leave their homey village for good.

Capt Ri's Parents

Ri Chung-Ryeol and Kim Yun-Hui

The loving parents of Ri Jeong Hyeok provided the stability that elders still look out for their grown-up children. His mother always served him with love, care, and support. She stepped in when his father's tendency for self-preservation over his family kicked in. His father's character went from a firm career military father to prioritising his family, despite the risk to his military status. The father's character was terrific and added top-notch humour to potentially serious, confrontation-laden scenes with Yoon Se-ri and Ri Jeong Hyeok. Furthermore, the same father eventually saved him from the jealous high-ranking military officer, who intentionally planned to kill him.

Seo Dan's Mom and Uncle

Ko Myeong-Eun and Ko Myeong-Seok

Seo Dan's mother and uncle were another set of characters that enliven *"Crash Landing On You."* Their riotous characters were much-needed balance to Seo Dan's fiery nature. Her mother was as equally fierce as her while her uncle continually normalised her mother's antics. Their equally clever bantering was overflowing with hilarity. The mother's character developed from being a wealthy and modern department store owner. Ever supportive of her only daughter, she eventually became a genuine friend of the ajummas from the military village. She remained supportive of Dan in whichever choice makes her happy. The uncle, who is such a funny man, has helped Ri Jeong Hyeok in many ways and continuously displayed his practical approach to life matters. These characters made the story complete but were a real treat to the viewers with their larger-than-life disposition.

* * *

Three

The Consummate Cast

The powerhouse performance of the cast of *"Crash Landing On You"* was a fine display of refined acting prowess, limitless energy and unparalleled charisma. The series cast cleverly balanced the demands of a kilig romance, heart-pumping action, witty comedy, and tear-stirring drama in a Korean drama series. The immensely talented cast deserved the highest praise for allowing the audience to feel an equal ounce of sympathy and contempt for the characters, for selling us moments of comedy and heartache, often in the same breath. The casting team exuded years of experience and pure luck to gather all these great actors in one blockbuster TV series. None of the actors felt stranded in the wrong part, a testament to casting team's exceptional judgement. The stars have aligned this series for all the genius performances paraded in one neat Korean drama package.

The National Treasure of the North - Hyun Bin

as Ri Jeong Hyeok/Captain Ri (Lee)

Hyun Bin was born to play the ultimate role of Ri Jeong Hyeok/Captain Ri (Lee). Categorically speaking, no other actor could have been as potent as he was as Captain Ri (Lee). He effectively captured the steely disposition and adept military skills in the action scenes that introduced his character in episode 1. Though thoroughly recognisable as Hallyu male star, it was not easy to distinguish between Hyun Bin and Ri Jeong Hyeok's introverted nature in the series. Ri Jeong Hyeok's deep-seated loneliness came through as he recited ten words to the tomato plant. He effortlessly brought it out from within, not him merely acting the part. His balancing of Ri Jeong Hyeok's expressiveness and restraint made the audience want to know more about him.

However, Hyun Bin did not just fully embody Ri Jeong Hyeok. He elevated the character into a much higher plane. A male lead, who cooks noodles from scratch and fumblingly buying ladies' products, has never been this unforgettable. He also innovated the familiar pouty face that frankly should be trademarked under him for sheer originality. His comical timing was precisely on-point, not forced or exaggerated.

Furthermore, he turned the viewers into a sobbing wreck when he was unashamedly sentimental after Se-ri left North Korea. His many declaration of love for Yoon Se-ri was genuine and dreamy. The sincerity of his character appealed very much to the viewers.

Ri Jeong Hyeok is sympathetic but, being a North Korean elite soldier, expectedly taut. It followed that there was not much body movement to work on regarding his character. Still, he relied heavily on acting through his revealing eyes and his voice cadence matched his withdrawn character. In this 16-episode series, Hyun Bin created a nuanced character capable of delivering emotionally contradictory scenes. Some scenes viewers could not help but love and be smitten by him while a minute later, reduced into a sobbing wreck. Undoubtedly, Hyun Bin's portrayal of Ri Jeong Hyeok was undeniably convincing. He flawlessly shifted from delivering humorous lines to full-on action, then to unexpected kilig romance, tagging the viewers along the way.

"*Crash Landing on You,*" with its long 20-hour series, gave Hyun Bin a chance to prove how proficient he is and self-aware of his strengths and limitations as an actor. Captain Ri (Lee), popularised in Crash Landing On You have found Hyun Bin new legions of fans, who diversified in his filmography and other works after watching the smash series.

Below are some emotionally-charged scenes portrayed by Hyun Bin.

- In the scene where Captain Ri (Lee) confronts his father about Se-ri, where you could feel his emotion fully erupting for the first time as his fear for Se-ri's life mounted. He cannot hide all his frustration and worry anymore.
- In the DMZ scene in the finale episode, Ri Jeong Hyeok had to calm Se-ri down while also crying. Being the perfect guy that he is, gave her hope on how they'll meet in the future.
- The parking lot scene where Ri Jeong Hyeok, catching his breath, found Se-ri in the parking lot after being chased by Cho Choel Gang. The intensities of his devotion and fear were undeniable.
- The scene when Ri Jeong Hyeok was frowning and pouting over Se-ri's capitalist heart was priceless – full of absurdity that endears him more to the audience.
- When Captain Ri (Lee) ran outside his office after learning, Cho Choel Gang had escaped and moving toward Se-ri in Seoul. His grasping of air after losing breath to what he just learned is just so heartfelt.
- When Se-ri got taken, and Ri Jeong Hyeok ran into the woods desperately trying to find her. A couple of tears running down his face was a poignant, heart-wrenching scene.

Image source credit: Hyun Bin in the scene when Ri Jeong Hyeok realised he hurt Yoon Se-ri.

He turned *"Crash Landing On You"* into a timeless series. As proof, a year after its pilot airing, viewers are still re-watching *"Crash Landing On You"* many times over and still gushing over Captain Ri (Lee). Indeed, he is the reigning master of romantic Korean drama, who performed the role effortlessly. He turned Captain Ri (Lee) into a full-fledged cultural phenomenon worldwide. It is difficult to topple his highly regarded success as a leading man in My Name Is Kim Sam Soon and Secret Garden. However, Captain Ri (Lee) in *"Crash Landing On You"* smashed all those records and he did so with much swag.

The Picky Princess from the South – Son Ye Jin

as Yoon Se-ri

Son Ye Jin, giving life to Yoon Se-ri, could not be any more perfect. Whilst she's known for her superior acting skills in the melodrama genre, she has proven again in this series that she is the real deal, versatile actress. She delivered impeccable comedic timing. Her character is rather tricky to portray – a rich, self-entitled lady at the onset that the audience can quickly detest. But Son Ye Jin performed the character's nature with perfect balance, without being infuriating or irritating. She made it looked so easy. Even with the self-entitled attitude of Yoon Se-ri, her delivery made it all endearing and entertaining to watch. It didn't take long before the audience to root for her to overcome barriers, achieve goals, and end up with Captain Ri (Lee).

In the scene where she forced Captain Ri (Lee) to display public affection toward her, she showed a brilliantly thought-out, precision-level performance. Behind-the-scene videos revealed that Son Ye Jin studied her performance so earnestly and would have lots of ideas on how to execute the scene. Her crafty use of her ever-changing facial expression was always exciting to watch and never gets old. Her overall saccharine reputation coupled with her high-level of artistry rendered *"Crash Landing On You"* into a tour-de-force.

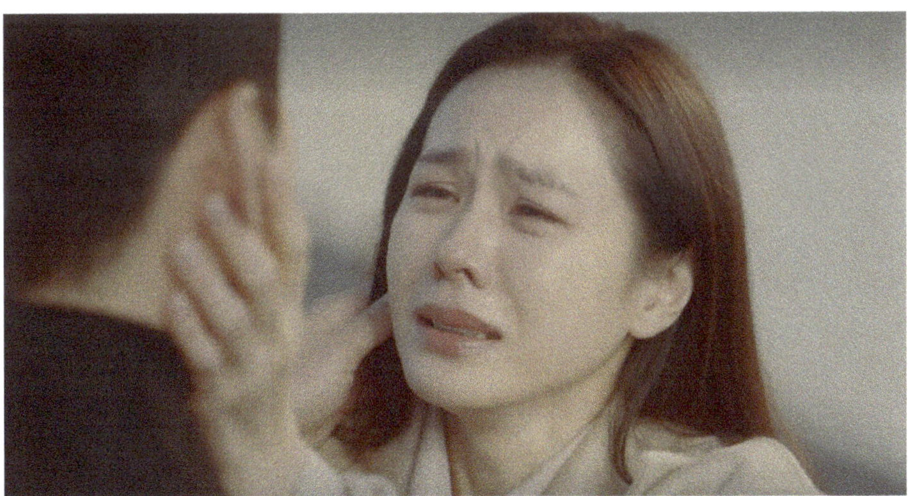

Image source credit to Netflix: One of the scenes that Son YeJin made audience cried with her in the series

Below are some emotionally powerful and memorable scenes of Son Ye Jin, where she ultimately brought down the house.

- She displays her refined acting performance as she almost choked telling Ri Jeong Hyeok of the "most beautiful ring she's ever seen." She promised not to take it off and ensured the dam of waterworks to come out in the open.
- The scene at DMZ during the finale: It was a superb portrayal when she was running, crying, and saying lines all at the same time, as she was desperately running towards Ri Jeong Hyeok, who just crossed the demarcation line in handcuffs. That is only the finest acting at its best!
- The scene where she gave out awards to the North Korean troops and a tomato plant for Captain Ri (Lee) – Her comedic timing was genuinely exceptional and adorably fresh!
- The scene where she was unboxing the staff that Captain Ri (Lee) bought for her, and then realising that Captain Ri (Lee) is sweet and thoughtful despite his uptight and dry appearance.
- Up in the hills overlooking the green lake, she looked and smiled at Ri Jeong Hyeok, which prompted a kiss. The finale scene imprinted in the viewers' memory as the fitting ending for Yoon Se-ri – a happy ever after with Captain Ri (Lee)!

The Love-Fated Couple – Hyun Bin & Son Ye Jin

Another highly-rated part of *"Crash Landing On You"* is undeniably scalding Hyun Bin and Son Ye Jin's chemistry. The explosive on-screen attraction between these two is exponentially more than any script could have defined their characters. During their first movie, "The Negotiation (2018)," with only a slight romantic angle, their chemistry was already out of this world. Their great looks are a special treat to viewers' eyes. But the comfortable bantering and jests resulted in a fun and delightful TV series to watch many times over.

One can see that both actors were precisely in-synced. They have a perfect sense of where the other was going and meeting each other at the right point, with the same level of intensity. Romantic sparks flew from the pilot episode, enough to ignite the whole minefield, where their first encounter happened. There were so many moments when viewers were carried away by the emotions delivered by these lead actors. Whether hilarious, heart-racing, romantic and tear-jerking scenes, all wonderfully and skillfully depicted.

Image source credit to TvN | Hyun Bin and Son YeJin created the love story of Ri Jeong Hyeok and Yoon Se-ri that swept the hearts of global viewers and brough the 4th Hallyu wave for Korean drama industry.

Both actors showed unparalleled acting prowess in *"Crash Landing On You."*. Both hailed as one of the most celebrated actors of their time, Hyun Bin and Son YeJin are the seasoned actors to play Ri Jeong Hyeok and Yoon Se-ri, respectively.

Some of the best kilig, romantic scenes of Ri Jeong Hyeok and Yoon Se-ri are as follows:

- Couple's ring. The series need not a wedding to signify a happy-ever-after. More effectively, it showed a scene when the couple put a ring in each of their ring fingers. More than an actual wedding scene, declaring their affection for each other through the couple ring gave out all the "feels" of a genuinely committed love.

- <u>Campfire.</u> When Yoon Se-ri was sleeping upright in front of the campfire, Ri Jeong Hyeok moved her head to lean on him in the backdrop of millions of stars.
- <u>First Snowfall.</u> A tipsy Yoon Se-ri inclined her head to Ri Jeong Hyeok's shoulder while watching the first snowfall in Pyongyang – what could be more romantic than this?
- <u>First Meeting in Seoul.</u> Yoon Se-ri thought she was dreaming when she saw Ri Jeong Hyeok one evening, standing and speaking to her in the middle of Seoul.
- <u>Picnic date.</u> In Switzerland, both were beaming with smiles and radiating joy, and a happy-together-forever in the end.

These two actors made their characters spontaneous and seamless as a whole. It is such a stroke of luck to cast Hyun Bin and Son Ye Jin in this series, given how the intricate casting process works where luck plays a hand. The handwork of the guiding fate was indeed written all over it.

** * **

The Fierce One from the North – Seo Ji-Hye

as Seo Dan

Seo Ji-Hye is the perfect actress to play the role of the fierce Seo Dan. The way she portrayed a ferocious character, who shall marry Ri Jeong Hyeok, by all means but eventually softened with Alberto Gu, was incredible. She carried a stylish, upper-class Northern woman who was every bit independent. Yet, she would weaken at the presence of Ri Jeong Hyeok, her forever ultimate crush, to which everyone can relate undisputedly. Her acceptance of things that didn't go as planned was such a moving exemplary. Ultimately, the audience rooted for her happy ending, too. She left a great impression of a chic lady who lived independently and learned that happiness was not solely dependent on a man. Such is the portrayal of a fantastic, powerful woman!

Image source credit to TvN | Seo Ji-Hye played Seo Dan's character, the elite North Korean lady.

The Charming Con-man from the South – Kim Jung-Hyun

as Gu Seung-Jun/Alberto Gu

Kim Jung-Hyun was the absolute one to bring life to Gu Seung-Jun/Alberto Gu. Though his character came from a wicked past and still embroiled in embezzlement trouble, he inhabited his role with lightheartedness. He served the right ingredients that successfully made Ri Jeong Hyeok jealous and a little insecure. He served as the Ying to the Yang of Seo Dan, balancing the intensity of their personalities. His feelings for Seo Dan drove his sorrowful realisation of his present condition. Him meeting some village orphans led to a turning point in his life, and he portrayed this perfectly. He did justice to his anti-hero persona, and viewers could not help but asked the question of why he had to perish. It signified a strong testament to how the audience loved this second male lead to wish a reasonable and forgiving conclusion.

Image source credit to TvN | Kim Jung-Hyun's character Geu Sung-Jun gave the audience' biggest cry at the finale episode.

The Unwavering Squad from the North

Yang Kyung-won gives so much life and spice to *Pyo Chi Su's* character, a master sergeant in Captain Ri (Lee) 's brigade. While he continuously antagonised Yoon Se-ri, he warmed up to her eventually, in the same way, he warmed up to many things South Korean. His continuous repartee with

Se-ri was a source of joy for the viewers. Their bantering came out naturally with their love-hate interaction. His portrayal of his character's naivete yet full of pride for his roots was nothing short of outstanding.

Yoo Su-bin, who portrays *Kim Ju Myeok* in the series, was another perfect cast. His character's fascination with South Korean drama stood out. His comedic timing was also one of a kind, and his character's mastery of South Korean culture through what he'd seen in Korean dramas was funny and memorable. After Se-ri gave them a hand heart, his facial expression was precious, and his contribution as part of the northern squad is priceless.

Lee Shin-Young, who renders *Park Kwang Beom,* a first lieutenant in Captain Ri (Lee) 's army, was a Captain Ri (Lee) in the making. With his silent type identity and stony personality resembling that of the captain, he was on his way to be the next Captain Ri (Lee). His character's lack of awareness and regard for his good looks made him more endearing and favoured. His portrayal and his nature seem to be one. One will hardly find it challenging to identify where Park Kwang Beom disappeared, and Lee Shin-young emerged in the series.

Lastly, **Tang Joon-sang**, who played the gentle lance-corporal *Geum Eun-Dong,* contributed his portrayal of plain innocence as the youngest member of the squad. He has a very young character, and his account of yearning for his mother was very heartwarming. His scenes with Ri Jeong Hyeok during a computer game is one for the books! His tenderness as he spoke of his lines straight through from the heart shone in the series. A truly bright future awaits such an actor with a tremendous passion for acting.

As a group, it has always been a fountain of happiness to watch their scenes as they exude openness to someone like Yoon Se-ri, who hailed from the opposite land, the south. While each character was very different, their combination as a team was very disarming and inspiring. They had differing opinions but somehow found ways to accomplish goals as a solid team. They elicited fun as a group where ever they were – in North or South Korea. These four were indisputably viewers' favourite as they depicted authenticity to their respective personas. Korean dramas are known to include a reliable squad, but this unwavering team from the North is going down in history as a top favourite. Undoubtedly, the audience wished for themselves such crew exists in their own lives.

The Staunch Ajummas of the North

A bunch of native ladies from the North Korean village ruled the neighbourhood's daily life. They were headed by **Nam Jung-Nan**, playing the wife of Senior Colonel, *Ma Young-Ae.* She was regarded as the most special unerring lady in the village and commanded the highest respect and servitude. Nam Jung-Nan played well as the "head", deservingly placed upon the pedestal by the rest of the ajummas. She also proved that she's deserving as the leader as her judgment guided them in times of trouble.

Kim Sun-Young proved her acting mettle, even winning the 2020 Baeksang Best Supporting Actress in TV, she portrayed *Na Wol-Suk.* She is the compromising village leader and one of the sceptical ajummas who disdained Yoon Se-ri after learning she's Captain Ri (Lee) 's fiancee. She and **Cha Chung-Hwa** (who played *Yang Ok-Geum*) had some indisputable sidesplitting comedy, such as when they reported to Captain Ri (Lee) that Se-ri was missing and the priceless reactions on their faces as he ran off fast to find Yoon Seri. **Jang So Yeon** balanced the group's mischievousness by being the gentle and kind-hearted ajumma, *Hyeon Myeong-Sun,* also the wiretapper's wife, Man Bok. She consistently threw in a positive spin for every cynical utterance from the group that kept the team somehow with a balanced perspective.

They spent some hearty times with Se-ri when they brought beer in her house after Captain Ri (Lee) 's fiancee showed up or when Yoon Seri was getting the 'goodbye hairstyle' hair-do. They shopped for clothes together, and when they went to the market, ending up hauling all the items from the pawnshop, all engraved great memories. Eventually, they all warmed up to Yoon Se-ri. Such a heart-pinching moment when they learned that Se-ri prominently featured each of their faces as the front cover of her cosmetic product line to let them know how much she missed them. Imagine the rambunctious if the ajummas ever set their foot in South Korea in the future.

The Great Spy from the North – Kim Young-Min

as Jong Man Bok

A raw and heartfelt performance of Kim Young-Min playing the craven and weak-willed *Jong Man-Bok* is also one for the books. The wire-tapper was a friend of Captain Ri (Lee) 's brother, Ri Mu-Hyeok. Though implicated with his friend's death as he was the wiretapper assigned to monitor him. His lifelong dilemma, being a passive accomplice of the crimes of Cho Cheol Gang, was weighing him down. Until Man Bok met Captain Ri (Lee) and saw that the same evil was being done to him as was with his brother, he then found the courage to face his misdeed and give justice to his friend's (Mu-Hyeok) death. His character had the most hardships in the series, which was also rightfully redeemed at the end. Indeed an organic portrayal of such a conflicted character with a touch of dramatic flair.

The Wicked Villain from the North – Oh Man-Seok

as Cho Cheol Gang

Oh Man-Seok, known as a funny guy off-screen, was the authentically remarkable villain in the series. His unscrupulous *Cho Cheol Gang* portrayal has left the audience wishing for Captain Ri (Lee) and Yoon Se-ri to win over his evil plans. Though his backstory as an orphan led him to be power-hungry, his portrayal as the ultimate bad guy made the audience believe his detestable character. The death of Man-Seok seen as the justice well-served. Only a thoroughly convincing account will make viewers hate a villain so much, and that's precisely what Oh Man-Seok delivered. In one of his interviews for the series, he reminded the audience that his character is just fiction and does not resemble his real-life identity.

Image source credit to TvN |Oh Man-Seok marvellously portrayed the master villain in the series.

Se-ri's Loyal Trio from the South

Ko Kyu-Pil (Hong Chang-Sik, manager), Lim Chul-Soo (Park Su-Chan, insurance agent), Kwon Dong-Ho (purchasing manager)

Yoon Se-ri's loyalists' circle is another group of actors that made the series so lovable and wholesome. Se-ri's life was devoid of close, trustworthy relationships, but this trio proved to be the most unfailing group of characters she depended on and looked out for her. When she was missing, these group kept searching for her and risked their life/work to send her necessary support, even against the wishes of some of Se-ri's relatives. *Ko Kyu-Pil*, acting out as Se-ri's manager, is to be praised for the perfect execution of his poker-faced dialogues, which were undeniably hilarious. The trio's marvellous portrayal provided a much-needed breather during the second half of the series, where the danger became too real for the lead couple.

The Phenomenal Mother and Spirited Uncle from the North – Jang Hye-Jin and Park Myoung-Hoon

Jang Hye-Jin's portrayal as *Ko Myeong-Eun*, a wealthy North Korean department store owner and mother to Seo Dan, was nothing short of fabulous. She's the ultimate doting mom who rightfully wanted the best and finest for her daughter, including her marriage to a military family's son. Her brother, *Ko Myeong-Seok*, played by actor Park Myoung-Hoon, was her source of much-needed grounding. A high ranking official in the military, *he* was a good-natured uncle and a laudable senior to Captain Ri (Lee). His practical take on things balanced his sister's scale, especially on matters relating to Seo Dan and Ri Jeong Hyeok. These two offer some of the chucklesome scenes in the series: the dinner scene in Dan's house, including how the uncle dragged Ri Jeong Hyeok to the apartment and the mother's choosing what to wear for the imminent visit of her future son-in-law. Both actors were fresh from their win as part of the Best Ensemble for Best Film, Parasite, in Oscars 2020. In *"Crash Landing On You"*, their contributions are most visible as they turned their characters into larger-than-life personas that the audience came to adore in the series. These two formidable actors showed their characters, and real-life personas co-exist within them - personas who are missed terribly after the series ended.

The Formidable General and Kind-Hearted Mother from the North - Jeon Kuk-Hwan and Kim Yun-Hui

The respectable senior actor, Jeon Kuk-Hwan, has played many roles in the past, but still brought new and exciting performance in *"Crash Landing On You"*. His character, Ri Chung-Ryeol, Captain Ri (Lee)'s father, placed high regard on his military position. He had to sort out his priorities as his only remaining son's life was on the line. His first confrontation with Yoon Se-ri was gut-busting, turning a tense situation into a light-hearted one. In the end, his character's love for his son won, and he became the ultimate saviour, though partly at the urging of his beloved wife.

Meanwhile, Kim Yun-Hui marvellously brought to life Jung Ae-Ri. Another reputable senior actress, she played mother to Ri Jeong Hyeok and wife and moral compass to CHung_Ryeol. Her tender nature was perfect for her forbearing character. She unleashed girl power when push came shoving, such as when she needed to remind her husband of what's more important in life. Her character's sympathetic and loving attitude revealed when she took care of Yoon Se-ri, whom she knew instinctively had a place in the heart of his son. It was so believable that Ri Jeong Hyeok got those compassionate DNA from her mother in this series.

The Entangled Chaebol Family from the South

In contrast to the warmth experience Yoon Se-ri had in the North Korean village, her South Korean family reflected the opposite end. A commonly portrayed dynamic of a power struggle in affluent families, tension runs high within the family. These actors and actresses showed us the complex nature of succession battles within a wealthy family. Yoon Se-ri's father, *Jeung-Pyeong*, played by **Nam Kyung-Eup**, made an unorthodox pick of Yoon Se-ri to succeed him instead of his two sons. This competence-based decision led his brothers, *Yoon Se-Jun* played by **Choi Dae-Hoon** and *Yoon Se-Hyeong* played by actor **Park Hyoung-Soo**, to intensify their resentment toward her.

Their wives (played by **Hwang Woo Seul** and **Yoon Ji-Min**) also pushed their husbands to employ worse tactics for the sake of winning the much-coveted power.

Meanwhile, the mother, *Han Jeong-Yeon*, played by **Pang Eun-Jin**, had a complicated relationship with Yoon Se-ri. She's not her biological child and a reminder of her husband's unfaithfulness. She eventually turned a corner and straightened out her love for Yoon Se-ri. They all depicted their respective characters with much passion as they delivered joy, tears, anger, hope and love to the audience that made *"Crash Landing On You"* a truly touching series.

Four

The Director's Refined Cut

"It is safe to assume that what we saw, heard and felt in "Crash Landing On You" was all a product of director Lee Jung-Hyo's refined taste."

While professionals and specialists support the director on these creative aspects, the director primarily gives the overall direction and vision. Production design elements, editing, cinematography, music and sound design, and other TV production parts must all obtain a nod from the director. He is one to receive credit or blame for anything about the series. Therefore, these are all reflective of the director's decision in collaboration with every department.

The cinematography was a very pleasing one to the eyes. Even in the North Korean setting, the soft lightning was enough to soften the scenes and retained the authenticity of a dangerous atmosphere. The locations in Switzerland were a such a beauty. Those captured the alps' beauty and the splendid colour of mountains, greeneries, and sunlight combined. It eschewed vibrant shades and flattering lightning that effectively conveyed a sense of optimism in an otherwise perilous scenario. The ending scene was made perfect by the stunning capture of the location that no one will ever forget and had made the series' finale exquisite.

Image source credit to Netflix: Scene at the demarcation line (DMZ) where many cinematic shots were shown that resulted to the most intense scene in the series

There's plenty of medium close-ups (MUC), and close-ups (CU), which is good as more people watch it in their small-screened mobile phones. It is a feast to the eyes when projected in a giant TV screen. The scene at the finale, where Yoon Se-ri was running towards Ri Jeong Hyeok in the middle of DMZ is an example. It utilised the moving camera so well that the audience felt themselves running with her in desperation. The sequence of scenes had cinematic features using deep focus shots and moving shots, to name a few. The aerial shot in this DMZ scene in the finale episode was almost like an art piece. It grounded viewers in the reality that two worlds are not ready to be combined anytime soon. It translated to the most intense sequence in "Crash Landing On You."

Another scene that posed a visual treat was the one under the stars. Ri Jeong Hyeok moved Se-ri's head to lean on him as she slept in front of a campfire. Stars peppered the sky, and the fire at the centre was like a painting itself.

The editing did a superb job as the cohesive flow of sequences avoided any confusion for the viewers. The use of slow-motion technique accentuated the dramatic effect of specific scenes. When Captain Ri (Lee) emerged from the underground office where the police interrogated him is a good example. Or the iconic slow-motion when he was riding the motorcycle, heading straight to confront the truck that was about to rampage Yoon Se-ri's car.

It was brilliant to tell a story within a story, and editing did a great job that never baffled the audience. Even inserting those precious epilogues was so great as that added richness to the story. The last word in one scene is cleverly connected immediately to the next scene, such as when Ri Jeong Hyeok admitted that he had a fiancee to the two soldiers, who believed otherwise. The next scene panned out to the arrival of the fiancee in the airport. Editing grabbed the audience at the start, took them on a beautiful ride of emotions and locations and swept them off their feet by the ending.

The series did not have those long shot of single scene, which frankly do more harm than good as it breaks the momentum and moments of boredom. Because theses shot focus on one scene (usually kissing scene) for 15-30 seconds, the audience is pulled out from deeply inhabiting the story to suddenly realising this scene is not believable anymore. With the absence of long takes, "Crash Landing On You" felt very modern and in tune with the audience pulse. In this day and age, people claim that they have no time for so many things. Thus, unnecessary long focus on one scene make the audience feel the waste of time given the 20 hours one has to invest in one complete regular TV series. The audience may think that their time is well-respected by the director by avoiding arduous long takes. As "Crash Landing On You" did not have such, the audience stayed oriented and emotionally engaged throughout the 16 episodes.

In the end, "Crash Landing On You" delivered precisely that, a beyond expectation experience. For a novice Korean drama viewer and a regular Korean drama fan, both were mesmerised by this series. Furthermore, all of these are credited rightfully to Director Lee Jung-Hyo, whose refined taste gifted us a masterpiece of storytelling that we cannot help but admire and love.

* * *

Five

Captivating Music & Soundtrack

While the visuals and dialogues of "Crash Landing On You" elicited a fantasy rom-com drama, the soundtrack of the series was on the side of the soul-stirring score. The musical score and sound design credited to the legendary **Nam Hye-Seung and Park Sang-Hee**. Both musical geniuses were genuinely responsible for buckets of tears shed watching this series and all the future nostalgia whenever these songs are listened to.

Some of the other musicians and artists that contributed songs are as follows:

'Sigriswil' is hands-down the magical song of the series, performed sentimentally by Kim Kyoung-Hee. It was the intro song that hinted at the light-heartedness manner of the series. But the same theme song, albeit its extended version, turned one's emotion upside down with strange longing in the very last scene in the finale episode. Amidst the gorgeous backdrop of Swiss alps, this song mesmerized the viewers as Ri Jeong Hyeok held Se-ri close to him but looked far into the horizon, almost looking to the future with some relief. This song indeed lingered and lifted our desire to want to see more of the couple. It went as far as to prevent viewers from 'moving on' emotionally from the series and from the characters they came to love unto the harsh reality that this series concludes as the song ended. Sigriswil was sublime, haunting, and evoked the longing of being together, side by side.

The song 'Hill of Yearning' by April 2nd accompanied the scene when the orphan boy brought food given by Se-ri and fed his younger sister, which undeniably pinched one's heart to a sad reality.

While the song 'Flower', sung by Yoon Mi-Rae, was rendered when Captain Ri (Lee)'s recited ten nice words to the tomato plant that made viewers feel reflective and yearning. The same song accompanied Captain Ri (Lee) and Se-ri jumping off with the parachute to escape from the military. When Captain Ri (Lee) searched for Se-ri in the marketplace while holding a lighted scented candle – viewers certainly partook in those romantic air. The song also played when Ri Jeong Hyeok realized and admitted to himself his feelings for Se-ri while he was looking at her while asleep.

Image source credit to Netflix | "Sunset" played along with this drone shot evoked so much feeling of loneliness at this point of the story, when both main characters have fallen for each other.

When the song 'Sunset' by Davichi played, it released certain gloom yet romantic atmosphere as Captain Ri (Lee) looked up at the starry sky as they both sat in front of a campfire while Se-ri's head was resting on his shoulders. As the song extended to the moving train scene on an aerial shot of a sunrise, the song exuded hope for the couple amidst the unfavourable situation. The same music played as Captain Ri (Lee) rejected Yoon Se-ri's plead for an embrace instead of a handshake, Se-ri's leaving with a broken heart.

Meanwhile, the song 'Here I am Again' by Baek Yerin surrounded the couple on their first kiss set in the hospital in the middle of the falling rain and watched the city skyline together during the first snow in Pyongyang.

The 'Song for My Brother' was the particular song that will always remind viewers of Ri Jeong Hyeok playing the piano near the blue-green lake. It is iconic in its own right. At the exact moment, the song also saved Yoon Se-ri from her depression and abandoning her desire to undergo euthanasia. No wonder many viewers also played this song when they could not sleep, seeing that Ri Jeong Hyeok recorded it for the same purpose for Yoon Se-ri's insomnia.

The rest of the soundscape and musical score were beautifully laid out and ennobled the emotions in every scene it accompanied. It is one of the most outstanding aural designs rendered for a Korean drama. I heard someone entered a PTSD-mode (post-traumatic stress disorder) whenever she hears any song from the soundtrack. Not just one song or sound, but all sounds in the series truly entered our foremost feelings and brought a rich emotional experience that otherwise would be average. The sound design of "Crash Landing On You" immeasurably accentuated the story's various emotions in its most distinctive and memorable way.

* * *

Six

High Production Value

Meticulous Production Design

Production design brings everything viewers will see on-screen. It includes small and big things in location, sets, costumes and makeup, and other items used to create a world inhabited in the story-telling. In "Crash Landing On You", it gave the audience a hardly-before seen life in a North Korean military village and how Pyongyang differed from another city like Seoul. Consultants who were North Korean defectors supported the production design team, which resulted in a more authentic depiction of the country, people, and way of living. Viewers are more likely to have insufficient knowledge about North Korea, and the production team took it seriously to enhance authenticity. North Korea still portrayed as a dangerous place for non-residents, but the show also characterized it as just like any other place in the world, with a mix of good and not-so-good people. The nuances of everyday living in the military village were teeming and brought the audience in poverty-stricken rural life, yet with similar values placed on family and community. As Yoon Se-ri adapted and adjusted to the village's daily life, including joining the favour of the ajummas, the audience also felt

55

at home.

The visual design was also influential in setting up the central theme and varying tones of the series. "Crash Landing On You" is a love story composed of fantasy, comedy, action and dramatic scenes, but with the two main leitmotifs of light-heartedness and precariousness. North Korean village sets were naturally dark and mainly used earth shades to reflect the overall rural feel. However, to bring out the series' light feels, the *mise en scene* sprinkled with red, blue, green, and yellow colours worn by the villagers or backdrops in the village houses or markets. Vibrant colours do not overly pepper it, but enough to soften the dark shades inherent to the military village location.

Image source credit to Netflix | High production value with several international locations used for the series.

The Switzerland scenes elevated the production value of the series. Much audience pleasure was from the well-polished backgrounds from this location. The costume design and makeup for the younger versions of the leads in those scenes were well-put-together, creating a unified whole. No other site highly regarded as the scenes shot in Switzerland. The scenes were an impressive spectacle of the Swiss alps as the natural background rang true to the romantic mood. It provided the perfect visual design for the happy ending of the series. The last five minutes of the finale was devoid of any word utterance. Instead, all the visual cues lined up neatly to deliver the fairytale-like happy ending - from a series of photographs displayed inside the undeniably inhabited villa to the picnic held outside watching the sunset over the lake by the hill. All done with visual design magic.

Seo Ji-Hye even won the 2020 Baeksang's Most Stylish Award for Seo Dan in "Crash Landing On You". Furthermore, all jaw dropped, including that of Se-ri, when Captain Ri (Lee) tried different suits in the department store. The styling provided the audience with pleasure. Se-ri's toned down outfits while in the village were still very stylish. Indeed, these contributed a massive impact to actors like Hyun Bin and Son Ye Jin to their respective characters by styling them throughout the series.

* * *

Seven

Beyond A Love Story

"Crash Landing On You" focused mostly on the love story that revolves around getting Yoon Se-ri back to Seoul. However, it still touched on relevant themes and timeless human values.

Mental Illness

Both protagonists suffered from varying levels of depression and trauma. Yoon Se-ri even reached a point of wanting to end her life through euthanasia. On the other hand, Ri Jeong Hyeok's survival strategy turned him into a life void of any purpose and warmth. Both suffered from traumatic events in their younger years. Moreover, before they met, both were living a life devoid of any meaningful relationship.

Image source credit to Netflix | This scene relates to the moment that main character, Yoon Se-ri, decided to live.

Importance of Family

The series also demonstrated the importance of family support. Yoon Se-ri had an unsupportive family due to the complicated power struggle in the ultra-rich families. In contrast, Ri Jeong Hyeok's family supported him, just like Seo Dan's mother and uncle were sympathetic and encouraging. On the other hand, Gu Seung-Ju's family was not present in his life. The story signalled that family could be found anywhere, not just within a blood connection. The four military soldiers became more than a family to Yoon Se-ri and risked even their lives to save her at one point.

Importance of Community

Similarly, the series showed that engagement with neighbours in the military village made Yoon Se-ri's stay not only bearable but fun and meaningful. Though it may not be perfect and not easy to get along with people outside the house, it certainly brings more colour to life.

Respecting Different Cultures

With a real-life pending war between North and South Korea, this fictional story proved that people might have more common things that they agree on than disagree with at the end. One can even find unlikely support and genuine relationship from the unlikely situation.

Power Women

"Crash Landing On You" featured major characters as powerful women. Yoon Se-ri, Seo Dan, all the mothers, the ajummas and even the sisters-in-law - all characterised as indispensable, modern women. They were all fierce, wise, capable, independent and a force equal to the men. It is influential toward more recognition of women's contribution to society.

* * *

Eight

Room For Improvement

A feature series review will not be complete without some potential room for improvement. While "Crash Landing On You" is a brilliant piece of our modern time, there are a couple of aspects that may or may not have changed the series' trajectory.

The Ending

The ending of "Crash Landing On You" was the most talked-about part and the most thought-provoking. The majority of viewers read that the couple only gets to spend two weeks every year together. That is how the transition last five minutes of the finale episode were perceived. However, a careful check of the last three minutes of the finale provided much clarity. The house's visual design provided much-needed clues to conclude that it was a different time than the concert scene from the last five minutes. The couple is out in the open and not discrete anymore in the picnic scene compared to the concert scene. It is then safe to assume that they live happily ever after together and not just two-weeks every year.

This treatment toward the story conclusion threaded a thin line between a satisfying ending and an awful one. The writer has proven that she concludes a series with some audience engagement in previous works. She may not dictate the conclusion nor will not make it very obvious, like in the series "My Love From The Star." Viewers can think of the meaning of the ending scenes and, therefore, make their interpretation. It may result in an unsatisfying feeling from the viewers after heavily investing time, attention and emotion. It might all feel suddenly a waste of time because it felt unclear. Some might think, if I'd want to think of my ending, I would have spent those 20 hours writing my own story than watching this series.

The other result is what happened to most viewers. In "Crash Landing on You," most viewers felt that it was so great as a series and with the "hanging" ending, the most logical ask was to have a second season. Many had to re-watch it because of that lingering feeling of not being able to move on. It bodes well for the series, but it was indeed a risky move to not clarify the ending and anticipate the viewers' reaction. It was a genius application of the Zeigarnik effect that viewers cannot move on from the series because it felt unfinished or unresolved.

Reports underscored a group that filed an official statement that accused glamorising North Korea, which might have affected the series' ending. Regardless, the fate of "Crash Landing On You" was written as a masterpiece, sealed and safely delivered.

That Crash Landing Scene

If there is one sequence that needs improvement, ironically, it has to be the actual crash-landing scene. Though that sequence signified it as a fantasy story, the execution could have been better. It felt out of place compared to the majority of the other polished scenes in the series. It was grainy and felt cheesy. There might have been more creative shots taken to signify that the storm mishap occurred and the protagonist indeed crash-landed.

* * *

About the Author

Loves good, neat storytelling | Loves Bartlet

Reach gnoeypeat@gmail.com to get a copy of *"100 Ways Captain Ri (Lee) Made Hearts Flutter"*

You can connect with me on:

https://www.facebook.com/gnoeypeat

www.ingramcontent.com/pod-product-compliance
Lightning Source LLC
Chambersburg PA
CBHW040158160726
48006CB00014B/1812